JUSTINIAN I

Byzantine Emperor

Kelly Rodgers

Publishing Credits

Dona Herweck Rice, *Editor-in-Chief*
Lee Aucoin, *Creative Director*
Torrey Maloof, *Editor*
Neri Garcia, *Senior Designer*
Stephanie Reid, *Photo Researcher*
Rachelle Cracchiolo, M.S.Ed., *Publisher*

Image Credits

cover (left) The Bridgeman Art Library, cover (right) Newcom; p.1 The Bridgeman Art Library; p.4 Bridgeman Art Library; p.5 Teacher Created Materials; p.6 (left) INTERFOTO/ Alamy, p.6 (right) Shutterstock, Inc.; p.7 National Geographic Society/ Corbis; p.8 North Wind Picture Archives; p.8–9 North Wind Picture Archives; p.10 (top) Bridgeman Art Library, p.10 (bottom) The Art Gallery Collection/ Alamy; p.11 Newscom; p.12 (left) Getty Images, p.12 (right) Shutterstock, Inc.; p.13 Bridgeman Art Library; p.14 Bridgeman Art Library; p.15 Bridgeman Art Library; p.17 (left) Getty Images, p.17 (right) Shutterstock, Inc.; p.18 Shutterstock, Inc.; p.19 Shutterstock, Inc.; p.20 World History Archive/ Alamy; p.21 (top)Shutterstock, Inc., p.21 (bottom) Shutterstock, Inc.; p.22 Mary Evans Picture Library/ Alamy; p.23 (top) Mary Evans Picture Library/ Alamym p.23 (bottom) Getty Images; p.24–25 Niday Picture Library/ Alamy; p.25 B Christopher/ Alamy; p.26 (left) Shutterstock, Inc., p.26 (right) North Wind Picture Archives; p.27 North Wind Picture Archives; p.28 Shutterstock, Inc.; p.29 (top) Newscom, p.29 (bottom) Newscom; p.32 Bridgeman Art Library; back cover Bridgeman Art Library

Teacher Created Materials

5301 Oceanus Drive
Huntington Beach, CA 92649-1030
http://www.tcmpub.com

ISBN 978-1-4333-5002-3

© 2013 Teacher Created Materials, Inc.

Table of Contents

Justinian I

The Emperor Who Never Sleeps

Justinian I became the Byzantine (BIZ-uhn-teen) **Emperor** in AD 527. He was a powerful man. He dreamed of making the empire great. Justinian's wife, Theodora, ruled by his side.

Being emperor is not an easy job. There are many difficult decisions to make. Some decisions may appear cruel and unfair. Although he faced many problems as emperor, Justinian improved the lives of his people and helped the empire grow.

Under Justinian, a new **law code** was written that brought order to the empire. He made the Byzantine capital Constantinople (kawn-stan-tuh-NO-puhl), the most beautiful city in Medieval Europe. He built **aqueducts** (AK-wuh-duhkts), bridges, schools, and churches. Justinian's army conquered the lands surrounding the Mediterranean (med-uh-tuhr-RAY-nee-uhn) Sea.

Throughout his reign, Justinian worked hard. He accomplished so much that it was as if he never slept. Because of Justinian's hard work, the Byzantine Empire became the grandest empire in all of Europe and West Asia for the next 700 years. After his death, Justinian would be known as Justinian the Great.

What Is in a Name?

While the name Justinian is not used much today, Justin is a very popular name. The meaning of Justin is *just*, *upright*, and *righteous*.

Where Is Constantinople?

If you look for the city of Constantinople on a modern world map, you will not find it. After the Ottoman Turks captured the city in 1453, Constantinople was known by several different names. In the 1920s, the Turkish leader Ataturk (AH-tah-turk) gave the city a new name, Istanbul (is-tan-BOOL).

Today, Constantinople is called Istanbul.

Birth of the Byzantine Empire

Rome Splits in Two

The Roman Empire ruled parts of Europe and Africa for about 500 years. By the end of the third century, the empire was in trouble. The Roman economy was weak. Many leaders were **corrupt**, or dishonest. Invaders poured into the empire. In AD 284, Emperor Diocletian (dahy-uh-KLEE-shuhn) decided the best way to save the empire was to split it in two. He hoped this would make the empire easier to manage.

Diocletian put one of his friends in charge of the Western Roman Empire. The western part included the city of Rome. Diocletian ruled the Eastern Roman Empire. The eastern part included the old city of Byzantium. The Western Roman Empire fell apart. The Eastern Roman Empire became strong and powerful. Today, the Eastern Roman Empire is known as the Byzantine Empire.

coin of Constantine

Diocletian

Constantinople

The Emperor Constantine (KON-stuhn-teen) laid the foundation for the Byzantine Empire. He built a new city where Byzantium once stood. He called his city Constantinople and said it was the "New Rome." In 330, Constantinople became the capital of the empire. To protect the city, the Byzantines built strong walls around it. They developed their own **unique** culture and traditions. The Byzantine Empire prospered for a thousand years.

Roman or Byzantine?
People who lived in the Byzantine Empire did not call their empire by that name. Like Emperor Justinian, they thought of themselves as Romans. It was not until the 18th century that the term *Byzantine* was used to describe Justinian's empire.

Easy to Defend
Constantinople had long been the **crossroads** for **merchants** traveling between Europe and Asia. Its location was perfect. It stood on a narrow **peninsula** between the Black Sea and the Aegean (ih-JEE-uhn) Sea. The water made it hard for armies to attack the city.

Social Mobility

Social mobility means moving upward from one social class to another. Justinian and his uncle are good examples of social mobility. They were both born peasants but later became emperors.

Patricians and Plebeians

When the Romans established a Republic in 509 BC, Roman society was divided into classes. The upper class was known as patricians. Patricians controlled the government and the economy. The commoners were known as **plebeians** (pli-BEE-uhnz). At first, plebeians had little power. Over time, they gained more rights. Still, social rules kept the classes separate.

Petrus Sabbatius: A Humble Beginning

Petrus Sabbatius's (suh-BAT-ee-uhs-iz) uncle left his **peasant** family and traveled to Constantinople in search of a better life. He took a job in the army and soon became the leader of the palace guard. When the emperor of the Byzantine Empire died in 518, Petrus's uncle took over. He was now the new ruler! He had risen from peasant to emperor of the Byzantine Empire.

Petrus's uncle was an old man and had no son of his own when he became emperor. Petrus came to Constantinople to be near his uncle.

Theodora

Petrus was hard working and full of life and his uncle made sure that Petrus received the best education. Petrus was thankful that his uncle helped him. Since Petrus's uncle's name was Justin, Petrus changed his name to Justinian as a sign of respect.

Justinian met a young, beautiful actress named Theodora and fell in love with her. At this time, marriage between a **patrician** (puh-TRISH-uhn) and an actress was forbidden. But Justinian persuaded his uncle to allow them to marry.

When Justinian's uncle died in 527, Justinian became the emperor. Together, Justinian I and Theodora would rule the Byzantine Empire for almost 40 years.

Justinian and his council

Justinian's Code

For hundreds of years, Roman laws were written in books and tablets. The laws were good, but they were difficult for people to understand. Justinian wanted to make it easier for people to know and follow these laws.

Justinian hired a group of men with special knowledge of the laws. He asked them to gather together all the Roman laws. They rewrote the laws to make them easier to understand and got rid of laws that were outdated. Justinian's legal experts put the laws in an order that made sense. This new system of laws was written in one book. It was called *The Body of Civil Law*. This new law book was known as Justinian's Code.

Justinian made new laws, too. Theodora helped Justinian and encouraged him to make laws that were fair to women. The new laws gave women more rights and allowed them to **inherit** property.

Justinian's Code was used for hundreds of years. Other countries liked Justinian's Code so much that their leaders decided to use it, too.

Theodora and her court

The Institutes

Justinian's men also put together a collection of old law cases known as *The Institutes*. This collection helped lawyers understand how laws had been used in the past.

Marriage Law Under Justinian

Justinian's Code was strict in terms of who could marry whom. Although Justin allowed Justinian to marry Theodora, Justinian did not change the law for everyone.

Justinian's Code Today

Justinian's Code is still around today. Many ideas from Justinian's Code, such as "innocent until proven guilty," are included in modern law codes around the world.

Justinian's Code

At the Hippodrome

In Constantinople, the summers were warm and the winters were mild. The people enjoyed outdoor entertainment. **Gladiators** fought in open-air stadiums called *amphitheaters*. Wild animals performed at the circus. **Chariot** racing was a favorite sport of the Byzantines. Chariot races were held at the Hippodrome (HIP-uh-drohm).

The Hippodrome was the center of public life. There were races almost every day. The townspeople cheered for their favorite racing teams. The most popular teams were known as the *Blues* and the *Greens*.

The Hippodrome Then and Now

The Hippodrome was a horse racetrack built in a *U* shape. The racetrack was covered with sand and surrounded by about 40 stone steps. **Spectators** climbed up the steps to sit and watch the races. The Hippodrome could hold up to 50,000 people! It was decorated with copper and bronze statues of horses, bears, lions, gods, and goddesses.

Little of the Hippodrome stands today. It fell to ruin after the Ottoman Turks conquered Constantinople. An Egyptian **obelisk** (OB-uh-lisk), a fountain, and part of an old wall are all that remain of the Hippodrome.

the Hippodrome after the Ottoman Turk conquest

the Hippodrome today

the Hippodrome in Constantinople

The Hippodrome was next door to the emperor's palace. There was special seating for the emperor and his family. There was even a secret passageway that led from the palace to the Hippodrome. Justinian often went to the Hippodrome to watch the races.

The races were exciting and dangerous. Eight chariots, each pulled by four horses, raced against each other. Sometimes the fans grew angry when their teams lost. When the people saw Justinian, they called out to him. They told the emperor what they thought about his policies. The Hippodrome was one of the only places where the citizens could see and talk to their leader.

Nika Rebellion at the Hippodrome

Nika! Nika!

Justinian had great plans. He wanted to get back all the lands that had been taken from the Roman Empire. He hoped to make his empire the most powerful in the world. To accomplish these goals, Justinian needed money. He decided to get this money by taxing his people.

Many rich men lived in the Byzantine Empire. For a long time, the rulers had protected them. They had not been forced to pay taxes. Justinian changed that policy.

By 532, many people were unhappy and felt that the emperor was their enemy. When they saw Justinian at the Hippodrome, they became angry. Instead of cheering for their teams, they yelled in anger at Justinian. The people called out, "Nika! Nika!" meaning "conquer." The mob rushed into the streets and burned buildings. Then, they stormed Justinian's palace. They wanted to remove him from power.

Justinian was afraid and decided to escape. He went to the waterfront and prepared to leave by ship, but Theodora refused to go. She told Justinian she would not run away from trouble. Theodora's courage convinced Justinian to stay. He called in his army to put down the rebellion. Theodora had saved the empire, but many people died in the Nika Rebellion and Constantinople was destroyed.

Theodora's Speech

The historian Procopius (proh-KOH-pee-uhs), in his writings about the Byzantine Empire, recalled a speech that Theodora gave during the Nika Rebellion. Theodora's strong words convinced Justinian to fight for his empire. "Yonder is the sea, and there are the ships. Yet reflect whether, when you have once escaped to a place of security, you will not prefer death to safety."

Nika!

Race fans usually called out "Nika" to root for their favorite team. This meant "conquer" or "win." During the uprising in 532, the people yelled "Nika" at Justinian. They wanted to conquer, or overthrow him.

Theodora convinces Justinian to stay and fight the rebellion.

Rebuilding Constantinople

A Glittering Jewel

After the Nika Rebellion, Constantinople lay in ruins. The angry mobs had destroyed the senate building and the public baths. They had also damaged part of Justinian's palace. Churches had been reduced to piles of ash. Justinian was upset to see his once beautiful city in such bad shape. He decided it was time to rebuild. He wanted to make Constantinople bigger and better than ever.

Justinian wanted Constantinople to be a glittering jewel. He also wanted the people to be happy and safe there. Justinian called in **architects** and builders from across the empire. Everyone went to work.

New buildings seemed to spring up over night. New aqueducts brought fresh water down from the forests. New bridges were constructed over waterways.

Hospitals and **orphanages** were built around the empire. The orphanages gave children without parents or homes a safe place to live. Schools were built so that people could be educated. Many new churches now stood in the city.

The defensive walls were strengthened. This helped to keep the empire safe from attacks. Everything, including Justinian's palace and the senate building, was repaired. Constantinople had been successfully restored to its former glory.

Constantinople

The Basilica Cistern

Justinian had an underground **cistern** (SIS-tern) built to store water for the people's needs. By the 1540s, the cistern had been mostly forgotten. That is when a French explorer found what he thought was an underground lake. It turned out to be Justinian's cistern!

Roman Aqueducts

Roman engineers designed a way to bring water from the forests and mountains into the cities. These water systems were called *aqueducts*. The aqueduct system used gravity to move water to where it was needed. It made fresh running water available for public use.

aqueducts

The Hagia Sophia

Constantinople had long been a Christian city. Byzantine emperors had built many churches there over the years. During the Nika Rebellion, some of the old churches were destroyed. One church, the Hagia Sophia (AI-yuh SOH-fi-uh), was the most important building in the empire. Justinian wanted to rebuild the great church on a grand scale.

inside the Hagia Sophia

outside the Hagia Sophia

Build It Fast!

Justinian ordered 10,000 men to work on the Hagia Sophia. He visited the building site every day and encouraged the workers to race against each other to finish the church quickly. It took only six years to complete the project.

An Artistic Wonder

Artisans were hired to turn the Hagia Sophia into an artistic wonder. Building materials were brought in from around the empire, including gold from Egypt, white marble from Greece, and precious stones from North Africa.

Justinian wanted the church to be the symbol of his power. More importantly, he wanted it to be the symbol of God's power. Justinian hired two engineers to design this new centerpiece for his empire. He told them that it did not matter how much it cost. All that mattered was that the church be finished quickly. Justinian wanted the glory of the new church to belong to him, not a future emperor.

The engineers did not disappoint Justinian. When completed, the church was remarkable. It was unlike any other church at that time. It had the largest unsupported dome in the world. The weight of the vast dome was spread over other half-domes and full domes called *cupolas* (KYOO-puh-luhz). It was awe-inspiring.

Justinian and the Arts

Justinian was a **patron**, or supporter, of the arts. He encouraged artists to develop new techniques. Byzantine art grew from the art of ancient Greece. Byzantine art pieces were famous throughout the world.

Mosaics (moh-ZEY-iks) had been used by the Romans to decorate floors. Mosaics are pictures made from small colored pieces of glass or stone. Beginning in the fifth century, Byzantine artists used mosaics on walls and ceilings. Justinian's artists learned to set the tiles in a way that reflected the light. This made the artwork sparkle.

Byzantine gold and silversmiths created beautiful jewelry. Justinian's artists also made carvings from **ivory**. Several of these ivory carvings showed Justinian on a horse. These symbolized his many military victories.

Justinian supported religious art, as well. **Icon** art was very popular at this time. An icon is a religious image. According to Byzantine religious traditions, icons allowed people to make direct contact with those whose images were on the icons. People addressed their prayers to them. Icons were thought to be powerful. They could bring about miracles and healing. The figures of the Christian Church—Jesus, Mary, and the apostles—were the main focus of icon art.

Byzantine ivory art

mosaic of Jesus Christ in the Hagia Sophia

The Power of the Icon

Byzantine icon making was a big business. Icons ranged in size from small to monumental. Some icons were made as necklaces. Other icons were like small books that could be opened. Icons were even used by armies. They would carry them into battle for protection. Inside churches, entire ceilings were turned into icons when they were painted with religious themes.

Iconoclasm

Long after Justinian's death, rulers of the Byzantine Empire made the use of icons illegal. This was called *iconoclasm* (ahy-KON-uh-klaz-uhm). People destroyed many icons and covered over religious paintings in churches. After 843, icons were allowed again.

Byzantine mosaic

Regaining an Empire

Justinian thought of himself as the ruler of the Roman Empire. But, the Western Empire had fallen into the hands of invaders. The Vandals had taken over North Africa. Justinian wanted it back. To do this, he would need the help of a great military leader.

General Belisarius (bel-uh-SAIR-ee-uhs) had saved Constantinople during the Nika Rebellion. In 533, Belisarius and his soldiers fought the Vandals and won control of North Africa. When Belisarius returned to Constantinople, Justinian held a special celebration for him. It was called a ***triumph***. Everyone celebrated Belisarius and his victory.

the triumph of Belisarius

War with Persia

Persia and Rome were bitter enemies. These two nations engaged in warfare longer than any other nations in all of world history. After the Roman Empire split, the Byzantine Empire continued the rivalry. From 53 BC to AD 627, the Byzantine Empire and Persia fought almost constantly.

A Triumph

A triumph was a public celebration for a military victory. During Belisarius's triumph, the people cheered as he walked through the streets of the city and into the Hippodrome. The triumph was a way to thank Belisarius for his loyalty and for his victory over the Vandals.

Belisarius invades Rome.

Justinian then sent Belisarius to Rome. Rome had once been the center of the empire. More than anything else, Justinian wanted to rule Rome like the great Roman emperors of the past. Belisarius and his army fought for many years. They succeeded in claiming much of the land surrounding the Mediterranean Sea. But the wars were costly. Justinian would need more money to protect the empire.

Belisarius

Justinian's Misfortunes

Struck by the Plague

In 541, a terrible sickness came to Constantinople. No one understood where it came from or how it spread so quickly. People suddenly became ill with headaches and fevers. Black patches appeared on their skin. Later this sickness would be remembered as the "Black Death." Some called it the Plague of Justinian.

The **bubonic** (byoo-BON-ik) **plague** arrived on boats from Egypt. It was not carried by people, but rather by rats with infected fleas. Thousands of people died. In Constantinople, as many as 10,000 people died each day for four months. No one knew what to do. The people who were not struck by the plague left the city. Constantinople seemed empty.

people suffering from the plague

bacteria that caused the Plague of Justinian

Yersinia Pestis

When the plague struck Constantinople, no one understood where it came from. It was not until 1894 that a researcher discovered the plague was caused by a bacteria called Yersinia pestis (yuhr-SIN-ee-uh PES-tiss). The bacterium was spread by fleas.

Social Effects of the Plague

Some historians think that the plague played a role in bringing about important social changes in Europe and Asia. Crowded cities lost many citizens to the plague. Afterward, there were not enough workers. Business owners were willing to pay higher wages to workers. Higher incomes improved living conditions for many Europeans.

Justinian became sick with the plague. For several months, no one was sure if he would live or die. Theodora ruled the empire while Justinian struggled to survive. Finally, Justinian started to recover.

Although Justinian had survived, his empire suffered terribly. Nearly half the population of Constantinople was lost to the plague. The economy was ruined. After so much success, Justinian's empire was almost completely destroyed by a tiny insect.

Another Tragedy

In December 557, a terrible earthquake struck Constantinople. The huge dome of the Hagia Sophia was weakened by the shaking. Months later in May 558, the entire dome collapsed.

The Theodosian Walls

The Theodosian Walls, built in 432, protected the city of Constantinople for over a thousand years. The citizens of the city were asked to help build the walls. They were happy to help. They wanted to protect their families and property from invaders.

More Problems for Justinian

Constantinople struggled back to life after the plague. General Belisarius went out to conquer more lands and Justinian slowly recovered from his sickness. But in 548, a great tragedy struck Justinian. Theodora died.

Justinian and Theodora

the Theodosian Walls

The Huns invade Europe.

Theodora had done many important things for the Byzantine people, especially for women. She had helped make new laws that protected women's rights. Because of her work, women of the Byzantine Empire had greater **equality** than women in other parts of Europe. Theodora also gave Justinian the courage to be strong. For the next 17 years, he would have to rule without her.

The size of Justinian's empire had doubled. But because of the plague, Justinian's army was less than half its former size. The army could not hold onto all of the new lands. In 559, the **Huns**, invaders from the East, tried to take over. Fortunately, Constantinople was protected by bodies of water and its defensive walls.

On November 14, 565, Justinian died in his sleep. He was 83 years old. He had served his people as emperor for 42 years.

Justinian's Legacy

Justinian faced many challenges during his time as emperor. The Nika Rebellion destroyed lives and property. Wars were costly to the Byzantine Empire. Outside forces caused problems. There were enemy invaders, earthquakes, and the plague. Justinian tried to deal with all of these problems the best he could.

Two of Justinian's greatest accomplishments include Justinian's Code and the Hagia Sophia. Justinian's Code was fair and just. It protected the common people. Many countries throughout the world adopted it. Justinian also rebuilt the Hagia Sophia. Although it was damaged in earthquakes, parts of the original Hagia Sophia stand today. It serves as a reminder of Justinian's vision for Constantinople.

The Byzantine Empire would never have a ruler like Justinian again. Justinian's people remembered him as a great man and a strong emperor. He worked hard and accomplished a great deal. Much of the work Justinian did was for the good of his people and the safety of his empire.

the Hagia Sophia

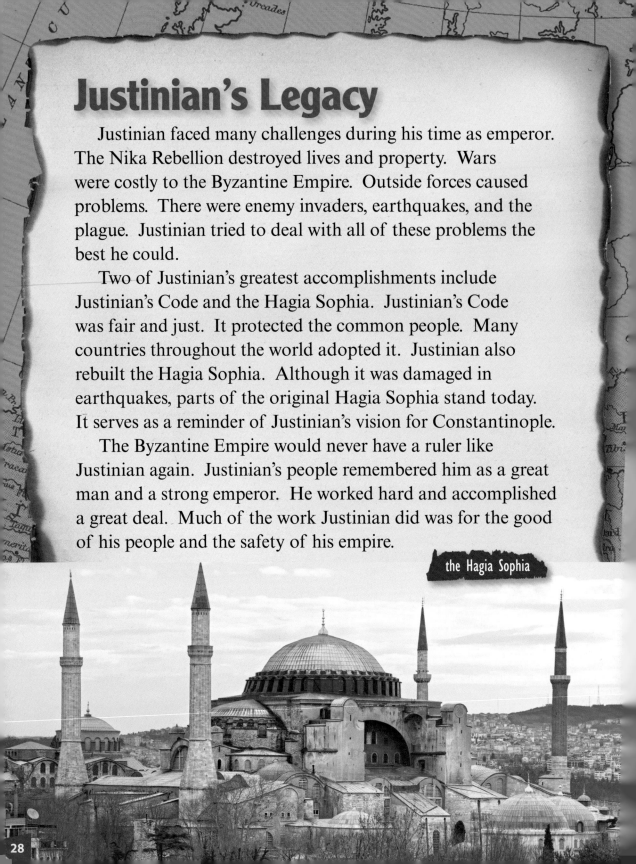

The Column of Justinian

The Column of Justinian stood next to the Hagia Sophia. It was as tall as the dome of the church. The column was made of brick. On top of the column stood a bronze statue of Justinian on a horse.

The Church of San Vitale Mosaic

Inside the Church of San Vitale (vee-TAHL-ay) in Italy is a famous mosaic of Justinian. Justinian stands at the center of a group of soldiers, clergy, and court officials. This shows that Justinian was the leader of the church and the state. Around his head is a gold halo. This shows that the people thought he was a good and holy man.

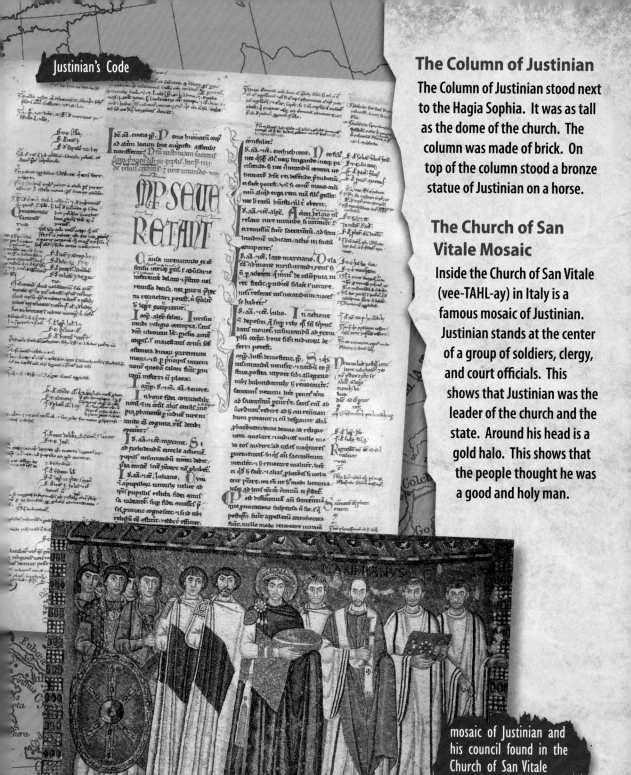

mosaic of Justinian and his council found in the Church of San Vitale

Glossary

aqueducts—bridge-like structures for carrying water

architects—people who design buildings

bubonic plague—a serious and often deadly disease carried by fleas from infected rats

chariot—a two-wheeled vehicle that was drawn by horses

cistern—a large space, usually underground, used for storing water

corrupt—guilty of dishonest practices

crossroads—a main center of activity

cupolas—domes covering a circular area

emperor—a male ruler of an empire

equality—the state of being equal

gladiators—people who fight to the death in a public theater

Huns—members of a warlike central Asian people

icon—an image of someone or something sacred

iconoclasm—a Greek word that means "image breaking"

inherit—to receive property as an heir

ivory—the hard, creamy-white substance of which elephant tusks are made

law code—a collection of laws

merchants—people who buy and sell goods for profit

mosaics—pictures or decorations made of small pieces of glass or stone

obelisk—a four sided tower of stone, usually topped with a pyramid

orphanages—places to house and care for children who have no parents

patrician—a person of noble rank, an aristocrat

patron—a person who hires artists to create works of art

peasant—member of the agricultural class

peninsula—a piece of land that sticks out into water and is nearly surrounded by water

plebeians—common people

spectators—people who watch or observe

triumph—a celebration of a military victory

unique—unlike anything or anyone; original

Index

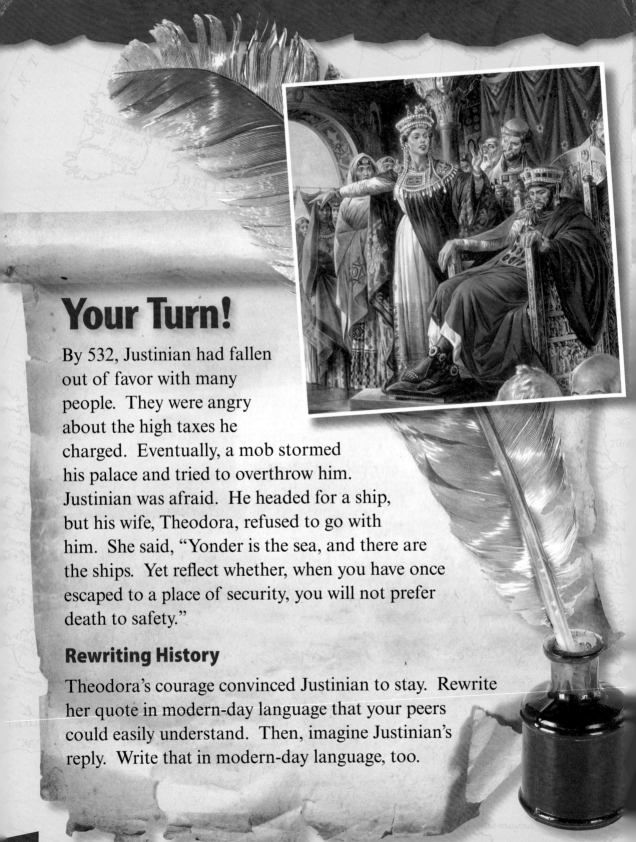

Your Turn!

By 532, Justinian had fallen out of favor with many people. They were angry about the high taxes he charged. Eventually, a mob stormed his palace and tried to overthrow him. Justinian was afraid. He headed for a ship, but his wife, Theodora, refused to go with him. She said, "Yonder is the sea, and there are the ships. Yet reflect whether, when you have once escaped to a place of security, you will not prefer death to safety."

Rewriting History

Theodora's courage convinced Justinian to stay. Rewrite her quote in modern-day language that your peers could easily understand. Then, imagine Justinian's reply. Write that in modern-day language, too.